This copy of

LIFT UP MY EYES

comes to

....

with love from

....

British Library Cataloguing-in-Publication Data. A catalogue record for this book is available from the British Library.

Published in the UK by Eagle, an imprint of Inter Publishing Service (IPS) Ltd, 59 Woodbridge Road, Guildford, Surrey GU1 4RF.

Scripture quotations are taken from various translations of the Psalms, selected with care to best convey the sense and mood of each individual Psalm. At the end of each Psalm the following abbreviations indicate the version selected:

NIV The New International Version
JER The Jerusalem Bible
RSV The Revised Standard Version
NEB The New English Bible

Typeset by The Electronic Book Factory Ltd, Fife.
Printed by L.E.G.O., Italy.

ISBN No: 0 86347 126 9

LIFT UP MY EYES

PSALMS OF GLORY AND HOPE

eagle

Guildford, Surrey

Blessed is he who delights in the Lord

Blessed is the man who does not walk in the counsel of the wicked
or stand in the way of sinners or sit in the seat of mockers.

But his delight is in the law of the LORD,
and on his law he meditates day and night.

He is like a tree planted by streams of water,
which yields its fruit in season
and whose leaf does not wither.
Whatever he does prospers.

Not so the wicked!
They are like chaff that the wind blows away.

Therefore the wicked will not stand in the judgment,
nor sinners in the assembly of the righteous.

For the LORD watches over the way of the righteous,
but the way of the wicked will perish.

PSALM 1: 1–6 NIV

How great is your name throughout the earth

LORD our sovereign,
how great [is] your name throughout the earth!

Above the heavens is your majesty chanted
by the mouths of children, babes in arms.
You set your stronghold firm against your foes
to subdue enemies and rebels.

I look up at your heavens, made by your fingers,
at the moon and stars you set in place –
ah, what is man that you should spare a thought
for him, the son of man that you should care for him?

Yet you have made him little less than a god,
you have crowned him with glory and splendour,
made him lord over the work of your hands,
set all things under his feet,

sheep and oxen, all these,
yes, wild animals too,
birds in the air, fish in the sea
travelling the paths of the ocean.

LORD, our sovereign,
how great [is] your name throughout the earth!

PSALM 8: 1–9 JER

The heavens declare the glory of God

The heavens declare the glory of God;
the skies proclaim the work of his hands.

Day after day they pour forth speech;
night after night they display knowledge.

There is no speech or language
where their voice is not heard.

Their voice goes out into all the earth,
their words to the ends of the world.

In the heavens he has pitched a tent for the sun,
which is like a bridegroom coming forth from his
pavilion, like a champion rejoicing to run his course.

PSALM 19: 1–5 NIV

The Lord is my shepherd

The LORD is my Shepherd, I shall not want;

he makes me lie down in green pastures.
He leads me beside still waters;
he restores my soul.

He leads me in paths of righteousness
for his name's sake.

Even though I walk through the valley of the shadow of death,
I fear no evil;
for thou art with me;
thy rod and thy staff, they comfort me.

Thou preparest a table before me
in the presence of my enemies;
thou anointest my head with oil,
my cup overflows.

Surely goodness and mercy shall follow me
all the days of my life;
and I shall dwell in the house of the LORD
for ever.

PSALM 23: 1–6 RSV

Teach me your ways

Make your paths known to me, LORD;
teach me your ways.

Lead me by your faithfulness and teach me,
for you are God my saviour;
in you I put my hope all day long.

Remember, LORD, your tender care and love unfailing,
for they are from of old.

Do not remember the sins and offences of my youth,
but remember me in your unfailing love,
in accordance with your goodness, LORD.

The LORD is good and upright;
therefore he teaches sinners the way they should go.

He guides the humble in right conduct,
and teaches them his way.

All the paths of the LORD are loving and sure
to those who keep his covenant and his solemn charge.

PSALM 25: 4–10 REB

Trust in the Lord and do good

Do not be vexed because of evildoers
or envy those who do wrong.

For like the grass they soon wither,
and like green pasture they fade away.

Trust in the LORD and do good;
settle in the land and find safe pasture.

Delight in the LORD,
and he will grant you your heart's desire.

Commit your way to the LORD;
trust in him, and he will act.

He will make your righteousness shine clear as
the day and the justice of your cause like the
brightness of noon.

Wait quietly for the LORD, be patient till he comes;
do not envy those who gain their ends,
or be vexed at their success.

PSALM 37: 1–7 REB

O God you refreshed the weary

When you went out before your people, O God,
when you marched through the wasteland,

the earth shook,
the heavens poured down rain,
before God, the One of Sinai,
before God, the God of Israel.

You gave abundant showers, O God;
you refreshed your weary inheritance.

Your people settled in it,
and from your bounty, O God, you provided for
the poor.

PSALM 68: 7–10 NIV

Shepherd of Israel, listen

Shepherd of Israel, listen,
you who lead Joseph like a flock;
enthroned on the cherubs, shine
on Ephraim, Benjamin and Manasseh;

rouse your strength,
come to us and save us!

God, bring us back,
let your face smile on us and we shall be safe.

Lord God of Hosts, how much longer
will you smoulder at your people's prayer?

Having fed us on the bread of tears,
having made us drink them in such measure,

you now let our neighbours quarrel over us
and our enemies deride us.

God of Hosts, bring us back,
let your face smile on us and we shall be safe.

PSALM 80: 1–7 JER

In the courts of the Lord

How I love your palace,
LORD of Hosts!

How my soul yearns and pines
for the LORD's courts!
My heart and my flesh sing for joy
to the living God.

The sparrow has found its home at last,
the swallow a nest for its young,
your altars, LORD of Hosts,
my king and my God.

Happy those who live in your house
and can praise you all day long;

and happy the pilgrims inspired by you
with courage to make the Ascents!

PSALM 84: 1–5 JER

He guards the lives of his faithful ones

The LORD reigns, let the earth be glad;
let the distant shores rejoice.

Zion hears and rejoices
and the villages of Judah are glad
because of your judgments, O LORD.

For you, O LORD, are the Most High over all the earth;
you are exalted far above all gods.

Let those who love the LORD hate evil,
for he guards the lives of his faithful ones
and delivers them from the hand of the wicked.

Light is shed upon the righteous
and joy on the upright in heart.

PSALM 97: 1, 8–11 NIV

Sing a new song to the LORD

Sing a new song to the LORD,
for he has done marvellous deeds;
his right hand and his holy arm have won him victory.

The LORD has made his victory known;
he has displayed his saving righteousness to all the nations.

He has remembered his love for Jacob,
his faithfulness towards the house of Israel.
All the ends of the earth have seen the victory of our God.

Acclaim the LORD, all the earth;
break into songs of joy, sing psalms.

Let the sea resound and everything in it,
the world and those who dwell there.

Let the rivers clap their hands,
let the mountains sing aloud together
before the Lord; for he comes
to judge the earth.

He will judge the world with justice
and the peoples with equity.

PSALM 98: 1–4, 7–9 REB

He satisfies him who is thirsty

O give thanks to the LORD, for he is good;
for his steadfast love endures for ever!

Let the redeemed of the LORD say so,
whom he has redeemed from trouble

and gathered in from the lands,
from the east and from the west,
from the north and from the south.

Let them thank the LORD for his steadfast love,
for his wonderful works to the sons of men!

For he satisfies him who is thirsty,
and the hungry he fills with good things.

PSALM 107: 1–3, 8–9 RSV

I lift up my eyes to the hills

I lift up my eyes to the hills –
where does my help come from?

My help comes from the LORD,
the Maker of heaven and earth.

He will not let your foot slip –
he who watches over you will not slumber;

indeed, he who watches over Israel
will neither slumber nor sleep.

the LORD watches over you –
the LORD is your shade at your right hand;

the sun will not harm you by day,
nor the moon by night.

The LORD will keep you from all harm –
he will watch over your life;

the LORD will watch over your coming and going
both now and for evermore.

PSALM 121: 1–8 NIV

The Lord takes pleasure in those who fear him

Sing to the LORD with thanksgiving;
make melody to our God upon the lyre!

He covers the heavens with clouds,
he prepares rain for the earth,
he makes grass grow upon the hills.

He gives to the beasts their food,
and to the young ravens which cry.

His delight is not in the strength of the horse,
nor his pleasure in the legs of a man;

but the LORD takes pleasure in those who fear him,
in those who hope in his steadfast love.

PSALM 147: 7–11 RSV

Photographic Credits

Eagle Publishing is grateful to the copyright holders, listed below, for their kind permission to reproduce the paintings selected to complement the text of the Psalms.

Cover	*The Sheepfold – Morning in Autumn*; James Thomas Linnell (1850–1905), © Bridgeman Art Library (courtesy Wolverhampton Art Gallery, Staffs.)
Page 5	*Bluebells on the riverbank*; David, Sherrin, (died 1940), © Fine Art Photographic Library (courtesy Caelt Gallery)
Page 7	*The Shepherd's Family*; Myles Burket, Foster (1825–1899), © Fine Art Photographic Library (courtesy Polak Gallery, London SW1)
Page 8	*A golden harvest on the south coast*; Alfred Augustus Glendening (1861–1903), © Fine Art Photographic Library (courtesy Fine Art of Oakham)
Page 11	*The Sheepfold – Morning in Autumn*; James Thomas Linnell (1850–1905), © Bridgeman Art Library
Page 12	*Solitude*; B Edward Warren (active 1860–1872), © Fine Art Photographic Library
Page 15	*A child at the doorway of a thatched cottage*; Helen Allingham (1848–1926), © Bridgeman Art Library (courtesy Christopher Wood Gallery)
Page 16	*Harvesting Corn*; Henry H, Parker (1858–1930), © Fine Art Photographic Library (courtesy Newman & Cooling Gallery)
Page 19	*Our English Coasts – Strayed Sheep*, William Holman Hunt (1827–1910), © Bridgeman Art Library (courtesy Tate Gallery)
Page 20	*Springtime*; Christian Zachs (1843–1913), © Fine Art Photographic library
Page 22	*A Hillside Cornfield*; John Horace Hooper (active 1877–1899), © Fine Art Photographic Library
Page 25	*In the Poppy Field*; Leon, Giran-Max, (1867–1927), © Fine Art Photographic Library (courtesy Galerie Berko)
Page 27	*A Forest Glade, Springtime*; Johannes, Boesen, (1847–1916), © Fine Art Photographic Library
Page 28	*Stags and Grouse*; Charles Whymper (1853–1941), © Fine Art Photographic Library
Page 31	*A Beautiful Summer's Day*; James John, Hill (1811–1882), © Fine Art Photographic Library (courtesy Hinson Fine Paintings)